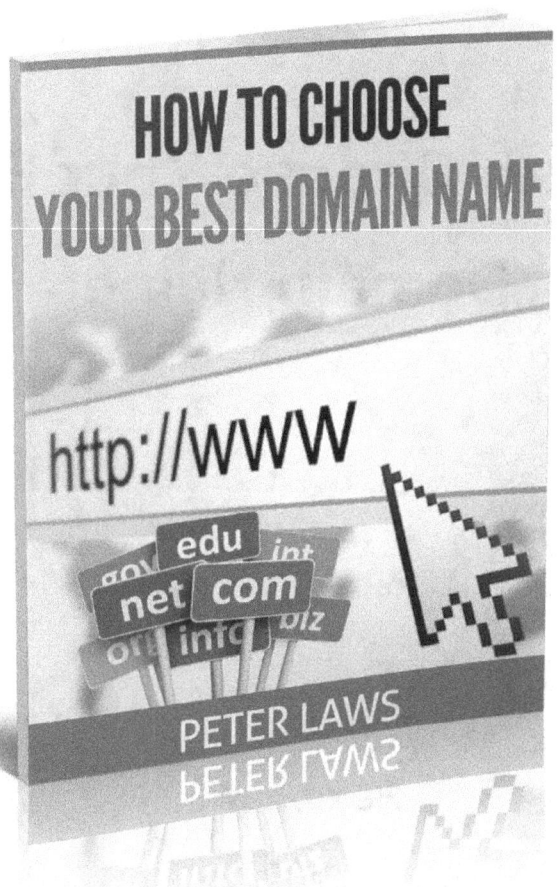

How to Choose Your Best Domain Name

by
Peter Laws
and
Gordon Goodfellow

COPYRIGHT NOTICE

Copyright © 2018 Peter Laws, Gordon Goodfellow

All rights reserved. No part of this book may be reproduced in any form or by any electronic or mechanical means, including information storage and retrieval systems, without permission in writing from the publisher, except by reviewers, who may quote brief passages in a review.

ISBN-13: 978-1729839768

Printed in the United States of America.

Published by
Email:

Visit https://www.popularpuzzles.org

Legal Disclaimer

THE AUTHOR OF THIS EBOOK HAS MADE ALL REASONABLE EFFORTS TO PROVIDE CURRENT AND ACCURATE INFORMATION FOR THE READERS OF THIS EBOOK. THE AUTHORS WILL NOT BE HELD LIABLE FOR ANY UNINTENTIONAL ERRORS OR OMISSIONS THAT MAY BE FOUND.

THE MATERIAL IN THIS EBOOK MAY INCLUDE INFORMATION, PRODUCTS, OR SERVICES BY THIRD PARTIES. THIRD PARTY MATERIALS COMPRISE OF THE PRODUCTS AND OPINIONS EXPRESSED BY THEIR OWNERS. AS SUCH, THE AUTHORS OF THIS GUIDE DO NOT ASSUME RESPONSIBILITY OR LIABILITY FOR ANY THIRD PARTY MATERIAL OR OPINIONS.

THE PUBLICATION OF SUCH THIRD PARTY MATERIALS DOES NOT CONSTITUTE THE AUTHOR'S GUARANTEE OF ANY INFORMATION, INSTRUCTION, OPINION, PRODUCTS OR SERVICE CONTAINED WITHIN THE THIRD PARTY MATERIAL. USE OF RECOMMENDED THIRD PARTY MATERIAL DOES NOT GUARANTEE THAT YOUR RESULTS WILL MIRROR OUR OWN. PUBLICATION OF SUCH THIRD PARTY MATERIAL IS SIMPLY A RECOMMENDATION AND EXPRESSION OF THE AUTHOR'S OWN OPINION OF THAT MATERIAL.

WHETHER BECAUSE OF THE GENERAL EVOLUTION OF THE INTERNET, OR THE UNFORESEEN CHANGES IN COMPANY POLICY AND EDITORIAL SUBMISSION GUIDELINES, WHAT IS STATED AS FACT AT THE TIME OF THIS WRITING, MAY BECOME OUTDATED OR SIMPLY INAPPLICABLE AT A LATER DATE.

Contents

HOW TO CHOOSE YOUR BEST DOMAIN NAME 2

COPYRIGHT NOTICE 3

LEGAL DISCLAIMER 4

START WITH THE SEARCH QUERY 1

DOMAIN NAMES 2

GET FOUND! 4

SEARCH NUMBERS VS COMPETITION: GLOBAL AND NATIONAL 7

SEARCH NUMBERS VS COMPETITION: LOCAL 12

AVAILABILITY OF DOMAIN NAMES AND ALTERNATIVE FORMATS 17

HOW PEOPLE FIND YOUR WEBSITE STARTS WITH THE RIGHT DOMAIN NAME 21

CONCLUSION 25

Start with the Search Query

Always start with the search query. Ask yourself, what would someone who didn't know I existed type into a search engine's search box if they were trying to find the service or product I was offering.

Put yourself in the mind of the person searching. What would they do? What would they search for? How would they behave? What would they type in their search box?

You want people to find your website by using relevant search queries; in other words, you want to optimize your website for those very search queries: these are also called KEYWORDS, and the main keyword that you use should form the basis of your domain name, because that is the keyword that your website should be built around and focused on.

This means that your domain name must comprise (or at least include) the main search keyword.

Domain Names

If you really want a presence on the Internet you'll have to have a good domain name for your website. Good domain names are important. It has to directly reflect what you do or what you have to offer as a product or service.

If it is a non-commercial website you intend to develop, such as one based on your interests, your hobbies, skills, family or whatever, then your own name will probably be fine for a website (if the name is still available - check first). But if it's for a business, a description of the business (e.g. LocaltownPrinters.com) would be better than a personal name, or the name of the business itself if it was long-established (e.g. J. A. Smith & Sons, Printers). Try turning THAT into a domain name: you'd end up with something like www.jasmithandsonsprinters.com. Not exactly memorable.

You could always capitalize the initial letters of each word (JASmithAndSonsPrinters.com), but who would remember that? Existing customers? Perhaps. But the real question is: would it be the natural thing to do to type that into a web browser in order to find a printing business in your town? Probably not. LocaltownPrinters.com is much more memorable. It also has a certain authority to it: you suddenly are THE local printing firm in that town: wherever possible, think generic (possibly with local connotations if you're providing a local product or service) rather than specific to an existing traditional name. (Although, of course, the business name may well have started off as Localtown Printers sixty years ago - so that's fine; it'll be well-known and memorable.)

Get Found!

If there's one thing every business owner wants it's for lots of people to find their business. This is especially true of the Internet. That's why you want a website presence (or a better presence if you have one already) on the Internet. The Internet, after all, is the World's biggest marketplace.

Forrester research reports that 85% of web sites are found through people looking up a related search term on the major Internet search engines. For businesses serving a local population such as your town, city or district, the same thing holds true. Potential customers and clients will still try to look up your business on their PC, laptop, tablet device or mobile phone in an effort to find what they're looking for.

Some businesses operate nationally or internationally, while others (especially mainstream service businesses) will operate locally. This is an important distinction in choosing a domain name.

For businesses which operate locally this will mean people entering a search term into their browser which will be the service or product they are interested and, plus their location. So if they are looking for a tax accountant in Cambridge they will enter (usually without quotation marks) "tax accountant Cambridge" or "tax accountant in Cambridge" or something very similar. This makes complete sense. So far so good.

So what you want your website to be found for is a combination of what you do + your location.

Similarly, let's say that you are a roofing contractor in Plymouth. Ideally, you will want **your** website to be at the top of the first page of search results when anyone types in any of the following types of search query into Google, or their own search engine of choice:

> Roofer Plymouth
> Roofing contractor Plymouth
> Roofer in Plymouth
> Roofing contractor in Plymouth
> Roofing repairs Plymouth
> Roof repair Plymouth
> Roof repairs in Plymouth

You get the idea.

Similarly, it's possible that your potential customer or client may search by postcode, or by town **and** postcode, so you will want to be found for all possible combinations of search queries which could possibly result in new clients seeing **your** website with **your** contact details, rather than those of your competitors.

You may want to narrow your locality to a district or suburb, especially if your city is large. This is especially true if your type of business is ideally suited to dominate small areas or if you only wish to supply a service to a relatively small local area.

There are elements in your website which will ensure search engines know what your site is about. One important one of these is the domain name of your site. You will want the domain name to reflect the search query which you want to be found for. I mention this now because this is where it all starts. It may be that you already have a website, but that it has an unhelpful domain name. This is discussed in a future section, but it is mentioned now because without the right name it will be very hard to optimise for the correct search query.

Also, if you are interested in attracting local business, there are Google Places and local SEO procedures to consider. But that is a huge subject by itself. At the moment we are only concerned with deciding on a domain name.

Search Numbers Vs Competition: Global and National

Now we have our shortlist of possible keywords/search terms from which we can derive our domain name. But how do we choose which one to use? For this section I will take a sideways step, as it is necessary to address two important metrics which, taken together, have a huge bearing on the choice of domain names from a list of possible choices. These two metrics are as follows:

1) Search numbers. How many searches are made for the keyword/search term in an average month;

2) Competition. How many websites are already optimized for that particular keyword/search term and how difficult will the top ones be to beat?

Let's try this out in practice by using an actual example. The local example listed above will probably not provide much data for comparison because the search numbers will be so small because it is so locally pinpointed. So let's take the search terms by themselves without the local keyword (i.e. take away the "Plymouth" and "in Plymouth"). We then have:

Roof repair
Roof repairs
Roofer

Roofing contractor

Roofing repairs

Now we can go to Google's own keyword analysis tool called Keyword Planner. It can be found at https://adwords.google.com/KeywordPlanner. You'll have to open an account with Google to use it, but it's free to open an account and use the keyword tool. We select the option for getting the search volume from a list of keywords. We enter the keywords in the box and select which countries or regions to target, then click the search button. The results are below.

Keyword (by relevance)		Avg. monthly searches	Competition
Roof repair		8,100	High
Roofer		4,400	High
Roofing contractor		2,400	High
Roof repairs		2,400	High
Roofing repairs		880	Medium

In the left column is the keyword search term, to the right we have the average monthly searches - this is the number of times the *exact word or phrase* has been typed into Google's search box - (in this case I have selected the United States and the United Kingdom together, so we have some meaningful data for comparison) and in the column on the right there is the estimated competition.

The competition estimate is based on Adwords, Google's pay-per-click advertising platform, so it is not going to necessarily reflect on organic search, which is what we are interested in here, although it is interesting to note that the immediate things that sticks out is that the less competitive keyword is the one with the smallest number of searches.

This is entirely consistent with the general rule that the more search there are for a given keyword (its popularity) the higher will be the competition, simply because more people will be competing for the more popular search terms.

The most popular search term is "roof repair", so we will want to use that keyword, if possible, in our domain name, in conjunction with our keyword location, in this case "Plymouth".

But what about the competition? Instead of relying on Google's estimate of high, medium and low, it would be good to get a more accurate snapshot on the numbers of actually competing websites. For this there are several software tools which can show this. For the analysis of competition I use a tool called All In Scraper (available at http://allinscraper.com/) which gives detailed competition figures across a number of metrics for each keyword search term.

I download the saved results from our Google test search and run this file through the All In Scraper. Below is a screenshot of the results obtained.

Keyword	AITQ	AIAQ	AIUQ	RCQ	Competition	Global Search
Roof repair	280,000	211,000	170,000	1,000	0.99	8,100
Roofer	354,000	165,000	178,000	1,000	0.88	4,400
Roofing contractor	313,000	102,000	131,000	1,000	0.86	2,400
Roof repairs	114,000	65,100	65,000	1,000	0.91	2,400
Roofing repairs	55,800	15,500	23,700	1,000	0.66	880

The first column shows the keyword, the second, AITQ, shows the number of web pages which exist on Google's index of the Internet have this keyword (again, Q indicates **exact match**) in their title tag (which is always a good indicator of how many web pages are actually **purposely** optimized for that keyword), the third column, AIAQ, shows the number of web pages which have links with the exact keyword phrase in their anchor text (the text which forms the hyperlink pointing to the site) and the fourth column, AIUQ, shows the number of web pages which have the exact keyword phrase in the URL of the page (the address of the page; the actual name of the web page or file).

The RCQ columns is based on the number of actual pages returning results from an exact search using that keyword but is probably a bit too complex to justify going into at length here (suffice it to say that 1,000 is the maximum competition figure which it is possible to score using this metric, which means that it is probably best not to try unless your life depended on it). The Competition column is a figure relating to Google's own estimates and the

Global Search column shows the search figures as supplied from Google already.

This data shows us that, if we were to build a website around the keywords above (without the location keyword as a qualifier) our competition would be almost impossible to beat, because the competition is so fierce. As a general rule of thumb, anything with an AITQ of over 20,000 will be extremely difficult to beat.

The above is an illustration of how to measure search and competition, and how these two metrics tend to be inextricable related: the higher the search numbers, the greater will be the competition. The above example would apply if we were to build a website based on a global market for the roofing business.

Search Numbers Vs Competition: Local

So let's go back to our local example and apply the same analysis to our smaller and less competitive market in Plymouth. Using exactly the same methodology as above, we go to the Google Keyword Planner and enter our list of keywords. This produces an output which I have sorted from top to bottom by search numbers, as shown in the screenshot below:

Keyword (by relevance)		Avg. monthly searches	Competition
Roofer Plymouth		50	High
Roofing repairs Plymouth		10	High
Roofing contractor Plymouth		10	High
Roofer in Plymouth		10	High
Roof repair Plymouth		10	High
Roofing contractor in Plymouth		–	–
Roof repairs in Plymouth		–	–

As I had guessed, these numbers are relatively small, and two of the keywords have not been registered in the Google search count at all, returning a zero output (though in reality there will have been searches for these; it's just that the search numbers are so low that Google considers them too low to record). Despite the low search figures, the local competition seems to be relatively high, so let's have a look at the competition in more detail.

Now if we run these figures on the All In Scraper utility we get the following results, as shown in the screenshot below.

Keyword	AITQ	AIAQ	AIUQ	RCQ	Competition	Global Search
Roofer Plymouth	532	3,380	141	199	0.76	50
Roofing repairs Plymouth	6	5	5	19	0.86	10
Roofing contractor Plymouth	651	60,900	225	65	0.79	10
Roofer in Plymouth	297	138,000	62	42	1.00	10
Roof repair Plymouth	1,410	83,900	310	54	1.00	10
Roofing contractor in Plym...	206	7	6	66		
Roof repairs in Plymouth	61	10	2	27		

Now let's export this to a spreadsheet so that we can chop up the data a bit more so that it more helpful in terms of what we are trying to do – i.e. decide on a domain name which will be based on a keyword which is searched for but doesn't have too much in the way of competition.

For this I have exported this to Excel and re-arranged the order of the columns a bit, starting with the search figures (as they're the ones that we are interested in to begin with – you do want to find customers!). and sorting by these search figures, the highest at the top.

Keyword	Search	AITQ	AIAQ	AIUQ	R
Roofer Plymouth	50	532	3,380	141	
Roofing repairs Plymouth	10	6	5	5	
Roofing contractor Plymouth	10	651	60,900	225	
Roofer in Plymouth	10	297	138,000	62	
Roof repair Plymouth	10	1,410	83,900	310	
Roofing contractor in Plymouth	0	206	7	6	
Roof repairs in Plymouth	0	61	10	2	

Now here's an interesting thing which immediately jumps out from the above chart: for some reason, the most searched-for keyword is *not* the most competitive search term.

Why this should be is unclear; there may be any number of reasons. But it immediately presents an opportunity for us. It means that we can build a website around the keyword search term "Roofer Plymouth" and know that there is relatively little competition. The keyword with the most competition, by contrast ("Roof repair Plymouth") has only 10 searches per month on average. So not only are we not interested in that (because of the relatively low search figures) but we also know that there will be more competition to try to rank the website around this keyword if we were to try to do so. So now we know that there is no point in targeting this keyword for our site.

We can also see from the above that the keyword phrase "Roofing repairs Plymouth" has virtually no competition, yet it has, on average, 10 searches per month, so it is worth our while in optimizing the website for that phrase (it may be on the front index page, or it may be one of the inner pages on the website which is optimized for that particular keyword). Even though 10 searches per month is not a large figure by any means, 10 a month is a credible figure for local businesses which, by their very nature, rely a lot on word-of-mouth. Also, bear in mind that some of your customers will be customers for life as long as your business remains trading.

There are other things which may be learned from these figures, such as the chances of getting the other search terms ranked as inner pages, etc. But as we are here to sort out which is the best domain name to register, the research done so far suggests that we should try to register a domain name based around the keyword search term "Roofer Plymouth".

Your choice of a domain name is an important decision; selection of your main keyword will determine everything else that follows after it. So it is worthwhile considering this matter again from a slightly different aspect. That is what the next section will do. After that there will be a factual section on which registrar to use and why, as well as advice on how you can get hosting discounts to make the whole process a bit cheaper.

The section which follows that will take us back to the registration of our roofing domain. So please bear with me; this first step is an important one and may dictate the success or failure of your website to attract new business without any further effort on your part, which is what having a successful website is all about anyway!

Availability of Domain Names and Alternative Formats

When registering a domain name with a domain name registrar it is always important to have the search term you want to be found for within the domain name itself.

For example, if you are an osteopath in Bristol you will want a domain name which reflects this. I did a check just now to see if the domain name osteopathbristol.co.uk is available, but it is not. Someone else has registered this name (and may or may not have built a website from it), so it is time to search to see if different combinations of this search term are available.

You can use hyphens in a domain name, so I searched for osteopath-bristol.co.uk but this was also taken by somebody else. So I searched for osteopath-bristol.com and found that this was available. It doesn't really matter whether you get a .co.uk or a .com name from the point of view of getting a good listing in the search engines. I just think that for a UK based business it is better to have a .co.uk name. But a .com name is also fine. A .org or a .net name is acceptable as well, but do bear in mind that .net names are usually used for Internet related businesses and .org names are usually used for organisations such as public bodies and not-for-profits as well as commercial businesses.

Domain names are not bought outright; they are registered for a fixed length of time for a fee. You can register a domain name for one year at a time, or you can register a domain for several years in one go, depending on the registrar you use. You can also get your registrar to automatically renew the domain at the end of the registration period so that it does not accidentally lapse. It should be noted that a .co.uk name is cheaper to register than a .com, a .net or an .org.

Some clients come to me with an existing website, but with a domain name which is inappropriate. Usually they have registered their own name as the domain, which is fine if you think that people who don't know you will search for your name on a search engine if they want to find your line of work (which they won't, which is a bit beside the point!). Sometimes this will work on an existing website, but usually it won't. Again, a decision will need to be made on an individual basis.

Sometimes a domain name will consist of the person's name as well as the line of work (for example johnsmithgardener.co.uk) and perhaps also the location (for example johnsmithgardenerboston.co.uk) but be aware that longer names are less memorable, and that people will **not** be searching for your name, but for your occupation and location.

Always remember that the best format for a domain name is [occupation] + [location] which is what people will be searching for; that is the format of the search query they will type into their search engine, and that is what you want your site to be found for, and the higher in the listings the better.

It may be that you already have a website and therefore that you already have your own domain name. In some cases these days when people buy an existing business they will buy the website that comes with it. In each case you will have a website with a domain name. So how does your existing domain name match up to the above requirements?

In general, all should be well as long as your occupation, or the nature of the business, is part of the URL of the domain name. For example, take the case of an existing business run by Oliver Smithson who is a florist in Derby.

If the existing domain name consists of [name] + [occupation] (e.g. oliversmithson-florist.co.uk) this will usually be fine. Keyword competition research will need to be done on this, though. Because remember that we need to be found for the occupation *and* the place name. Hopefully, in such cases there will be no need to register a new domain name if the competition for the place name is low.

In cases where the existing domain name consists of [name] + [location] (e.g. oliversmithson-derby.co.uk) then we may have a problem. In this case the occupation is missing. And, after all, it's the occupation that the searcher is looking for! Nevertheless, keyword research may show that competition for that occupation within the location is low, so we can make do with the existing domain name.

However, in cases where the existing domain takes the form [name] only (e.g. oliversmithson.co.uk) then clearly we have a problem. Neither the occupation nor the location is stated in the URL of the domain name. Keyword research will need to be done as before, just to make sure, but experience shows that a new domain name needs to be registered because the existing one is inadequate for the job. In such cases there may be no need to build a completely different website from the ground up – just to transfer it to the new domain

In some cases, where a business has been bought as a going concern and the name of the website consists only of the previous owner's name then the present owner will probably want to get a new name for altogether more obvious reasons!

Of course, if you have no website to start with then the problem does not arise. You can search for the perfect domain name based on the [occupation] + [location] criteria as described above without having to decide whether or not the existing name is suitable.

How People Find Your Website Starts with the Right Domain Name

The term 'domain name' is the name of any given website.

You must register a domain name before you can build a website for your business, and the website is called the same as the domain name. At the risk of repetition, let's have a few more examples.

Although the thinking behind a domain name can vary, most domain names will be based on the search words that people will use to find what they are looking for online. So, if the business is an electrician in Bedford, the domain name (and the whole website) should be optimized around these two words which describe function and location:

>Electrician + Bedford
>Bedford electrician
>Electrician in Bedford

because this is what someone will type into a search engine's search box when they are looking for an electrician in Bedford and don't already know of one that they already use. A website is always aimed at **new customers**. If the business is well established and has an existing trading name then it may be useful to include the trading name into the domain name as well (although bear in mind that the whole point of a website is to get **new** customers/clients; people who know the name of the business will also know the business already! It's the people who **don't** already know the business, but who are searching for what the business does and where it is, that you want to concentrate on, to get new customers/clients).

If, for example, a Mr Wilson and his son run the business, and if you have decided to include the existing trading name then the domain (and thus the name of the website) may look like any one of the following:

> www.WilsonsElectriciansBedford.co.uk
> www.WilsonBedfordElectricians.co.uk
> www.BedfordElectriciansWilsons.com

Of course, it is possible to exclude the location or place name from the domain name, and this may well be preferred if there are branches in several locations, and you want a name which describes the group of businesses as a whole.

When searching for the domain name to register for the business website it may be that the name you want on is not available as it has already been registered by someone else or some other business. In this case there are always alternative ways of getting a domain name which is approximate to the one you have decided you want.

For example, there are different domain extensions. So if the .co.uk version is taken then the .com version may be available, and vice versa; these days there are also .uk, .org.uk, .me.uk (not recommended for businesses), .net.uk (for Internet or tech-based businesses), .ltd.uk (for UK limited companies) and .plc.uk (for UK plcs).

It is probably best to opt for the .co.uk or the .com if available. If you opt for the .com then you are able to register that for FREE when you open a hosting account with InMotion, which is the recommended hosting service. Or you could get the .co.uk version if you prefer. At the time of writing 123-Reg were offering .co.uk domains at £0.99 for the first year.

If the domain name of your choice is still not available with any of the given domain extensions, then you can register a variant of that with a hyphen in it. Or you could put -uk in the domain, or HQ for a head office, or any number of combinations. You are only limited by your imagination.

    www.WilsonsElectricians-Bedford.co.uk
    www.Wilsons-Electricians-Bedford.com
    www.Electricians-Bedford-UK.com
    www.WilsonsElectriciansHQ.com

You're bound to end up with one which is both available and satisfactory. Now you have the name of your website. The site itself follows the optimisation course that the domain name has already started on: the search keywords are embedded and hard-coded into the structure of the website. The objective is to get the listing of the website to appear in the search results when someone types the search terms (the keywords embodied in the domain and in the site itself) into a search engine.

The hosting service is sometimes provided by the same company that you register the name with, but usually it isn't. Domain name registration and hosting are two distinct specialisations, so it is more likely that the hosting will be provided by a different company. If this is the case then the domain has to be 'pointed' at the hosting company by changing the nameservers at the registrar to the hosting company's own nameservers. The website's content, in the form of files and folders, is then uploaded to the host's servers.

Once this has been done it may take a few minutes (or in some cases a couple of hours) for the name to be associated with the website content, and the website will then be propagated across the entire Internet for everyone to see.

Conclusion

I hope that I have clarified what is not too difficult a subject. Of course, the matter does not stop there. Even though you may now have enough to go on to enable you to select your best domain name for your website, the process of getting your website up and running hasn't even started yet.

For that I can refer you to my other books (this time written under my actual name Gordon Goodfellow rather than the pen name Peter Laws) which are available at the same place you got this one.

My other books cover domain name registration and website hosting. The latter is quite a huge subject. You might like to delve into that one first, as the registration is relatively easy.

I wish you well in your Internet endeavours!